This book belongs to:

MY FIRST SAFARI IN BOTSWANA

Play & Learn

Activity book for kids

By Magdalena Collet

Can you find and colour Botswana on this map?

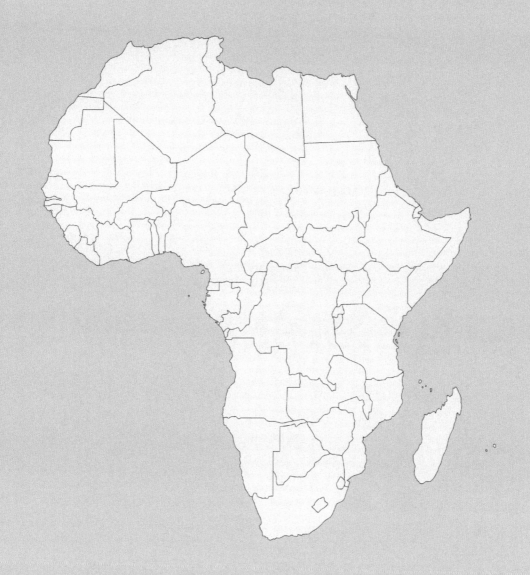

ANGOLA

ZAMBIA

ZIMBABWE

Tsodilo
Hills

Chobe
Nat. park

Okavango
Delta

NAMIBIA

Maun

Nata

Francistown

Ghanzi

Salt
pans

BOTSWANA

Kalahari
Desert

GABORONE

SOUTH AFRICA

BOTSWANA FACT SHEET

Capital: Gaborone
Population: 2.6 Million
Currency: Botswana Pula
Highest point: Tsodilo Hills (1375m)

Flag

National Bird

Okavango river

National Animal

Languages: English and Setswana

Hello! Dumela!

Pap & Seswaa

~THE BIG FIVE~

o Rhinoceros

o Elephant

o Lion

o Buffalo

o Leopard

~THE LITTLE FIVE~

o Buffalo
weaver

o Rhino
beetle

o Elephant
shrew

o Antlion
(larva)

o Leopard
tortoise

o Antlion
(adult)

~THE UGLY FIVE~

o Spotted
   Hyena

o Warthog

o Marabou
   stork

o Vulture

o Wildebeest

~THE SHY FIVE~

o   Porcupine

o   Bat-eared
     fox

o   Meerkat/
     Suricate

o   Aardvark/
     Antbear

o   Aardwolf

BUSY BUGS

○ Spotted joker

○ Dung Beetle

○ Fruit Chaffer

○ Velvet mite

○ Termite

○ Praying mantis

FLORA OF BOTSWANA

o Lucky bean

o Papyrus

o Wild sage

o Baobab
fruit

o Baobab
tree

o Devil's claw

TRACK ME IF YOU CAN!

Lion	Leopard	Cheetah	Hyena	Wild dog

Elephant	Rhino	Hippo	Buffalo	Zebra

Giraffe	Wildebeest	Impala	Kudu	Springbok

Warthog	Jackal	Ostrich	Crocodile	Baboon

GAME DRIVE

o Hippo

o Springbok

o Crocodile

o Giraffe

o Wild dog

o Kudu

o Baboon

o Impala

o Cheetah

o Zebra

o Python

BIRD WATCHING

o Kori bustard

o Glossy starling

o Glossy ibis

o Fish eagle

o Carmine bee-eater

o Ground hornbill

o Natal francolin

o Grey Lourie

o Ostrich

o White-backed vulture

o Secretarybird

o Red-billed
Oxpecker

o Helmeted
guineafowl

o Flamingo

o Great crested
grebe

o Jacana

o Malachite
kingfisher

o Bateleur eagle

o Lilac-breasted
roller

o Yellow-
billed
hornbill

o Red-
billed
hornbill

o Cattle egret

NOTES

NOTES

CROSSWORD

WORD SEARCH PUZZLE

B	R	A	H	I	M	P	A	L	A	G
C	H	I	P	P	O	I	Z	E	Y	B
R	I	N	O	U	H	M	J	O	K	U
P	N	Y	K	L	I	O	N	P	M	F
E	O	L	R	A	P	N	O	A	E	F
B	F	F	D	L	O	K	F	R	D	A
Y	U	D	U	K	Z	E	F	D	Z	L
Z	E	B	R	A	L	Y	S	Z	M	O

- Lion
- Zebra
- Buffalo
- Monkey

- Hippo
- Rhino
- Leopard
- Impala

COMPLETE THE VOWELS

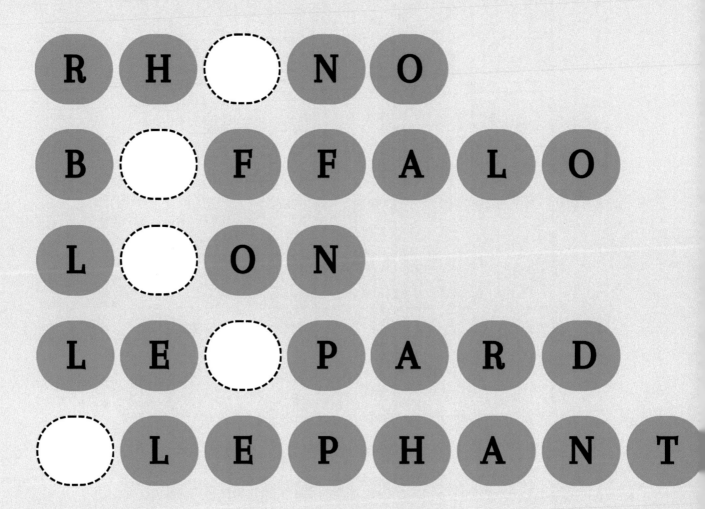

R H ◯ N O

B ◯ F F A L O

L ◯ O N

L E ◯ P A R D

◯ L E P H A N T

SPELLING WORD SCRAMBLE

Use the letters to spell the word.

G N A L

N P O I

⬚ ⬚ ⬚ ⬚ ⬚ ⬚ ⬚ ⬚

SPELLING WORD SCRAMBLE

Use the letters to spell the word.

L A K

C J A

MATCH WORDS WITH THE CORRECT PICTURES

MOKORO

AIRPLANE

CRICKET

NIGHTJAR

BUSH BABY

SAGE

MATCH'EM

Match each animal with the right track!

1 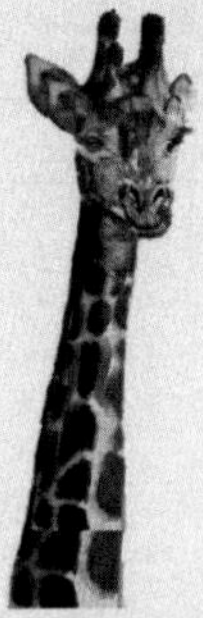

2 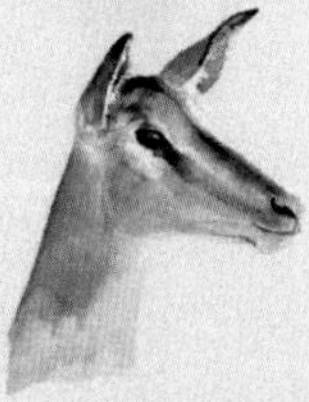

3 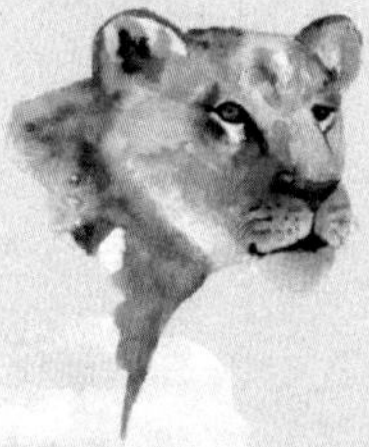

4 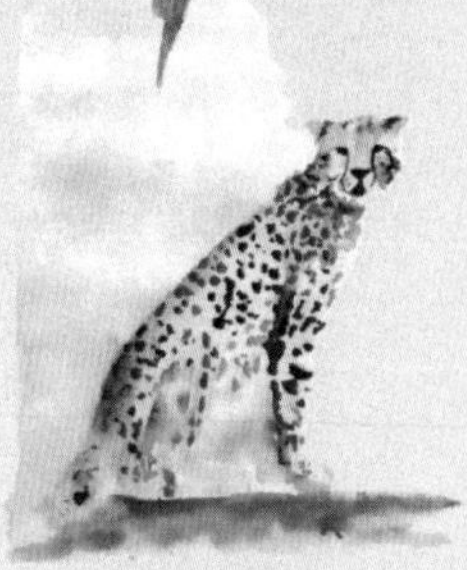

5 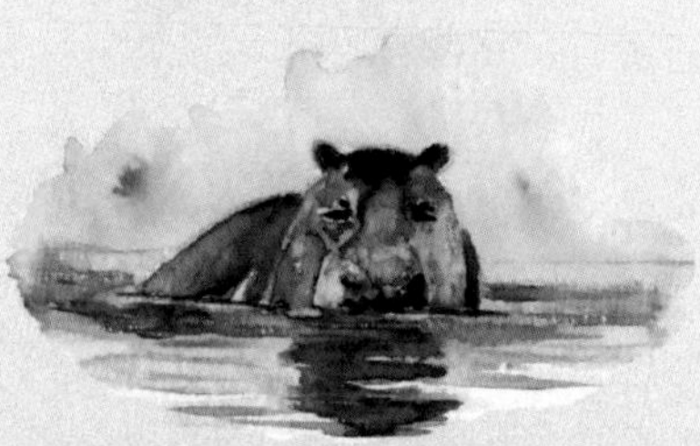

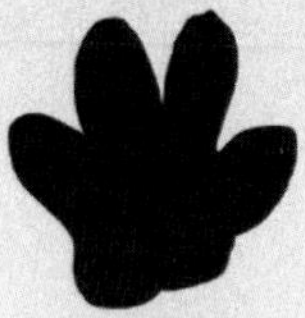 a

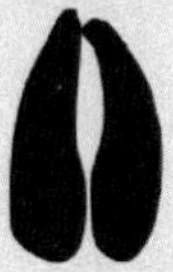 b

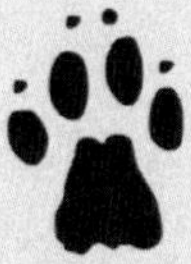 c

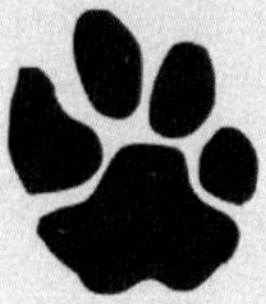 d

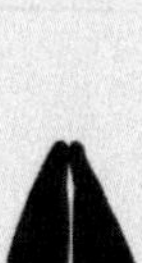 e

Answers: 1b, 2e, 3d,4c,5a

SAFARI QUIZZ

1. Which of the following animals is known as the king of the jungle?

    a) elephant   c) giraffe

    b) lion   d) zebra

2. Which desert covers a large part of Botswana?

    a) Sahara   c) Kalahari

    b) Gobi   d) Namib

3. Which of the following is the largest land animal in the world?

    a) elephant   c) hippo

    b) rhinoceros   d) lion

4. Which animal has black and white stripes?

    a) pangolin   c) leopard

    b) impala   d) zebra

5. Wat is the traditional greeting in Botswana?

    a) Hakuna matata   c) Dumela

    b) Jambo   d) Asante

6. Which of the following animals is not part of the big five?

    a) lion   c) rhino

    b) elephant   d) hippo

7. Which animal has a long neck and eats leaves from tall trees?

    a) giraffe   c) zebra

    b) impala   d) wildebeest

Answers: 1b, 2c, 3a,4d,5c, 6d, 7a

MAZE

WHO AM I?

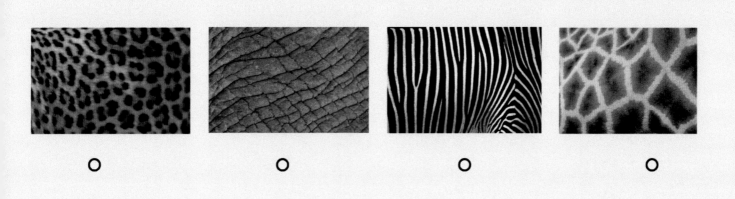

WHO AM I?

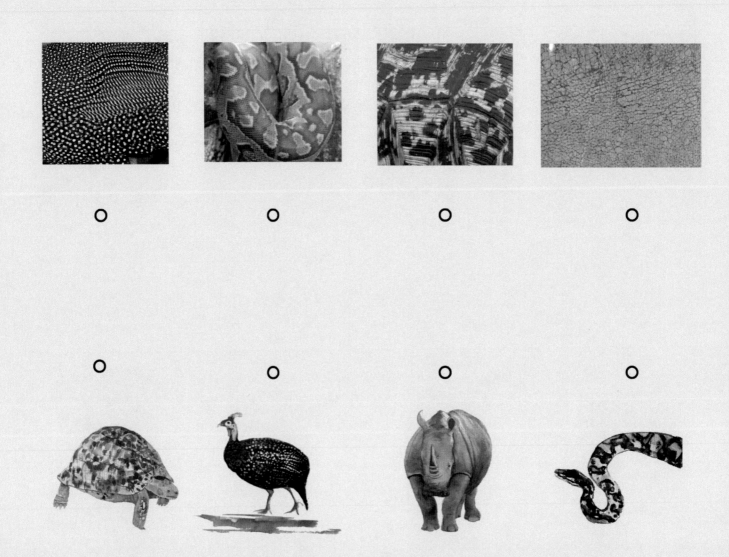

WHO AM I?

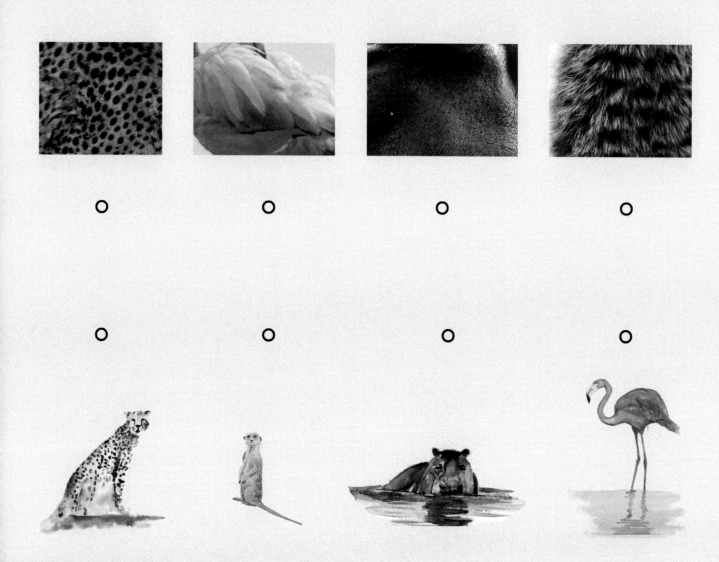

WHO AM I?

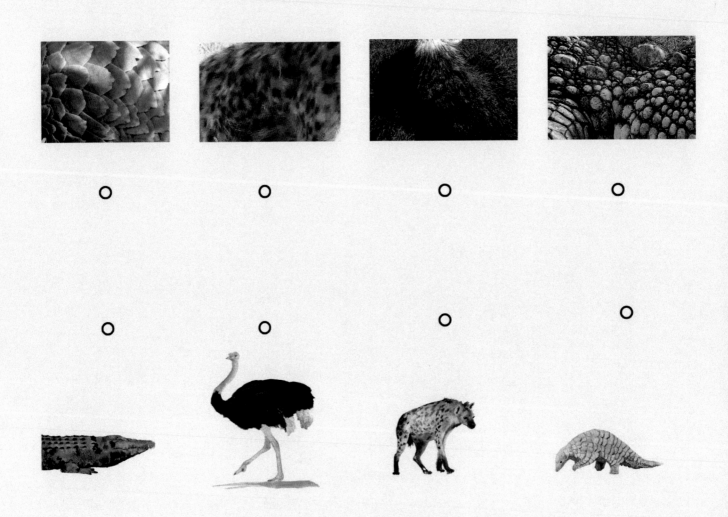

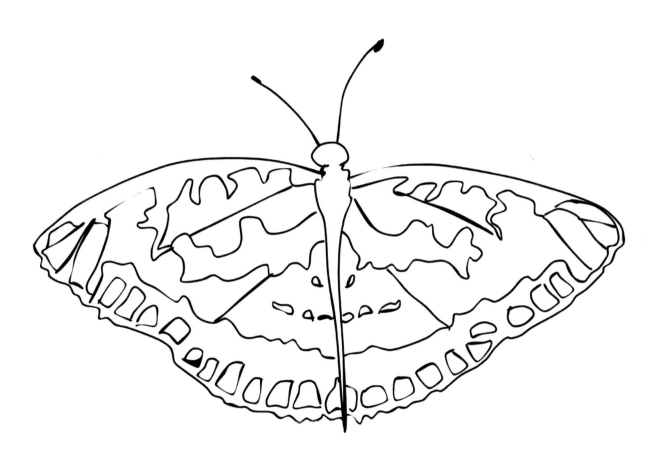

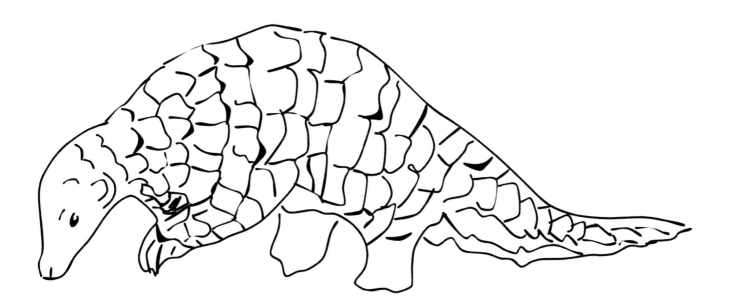

NOTES

NOTES

From the same collection

The Little Botswana Boy, Life in Savuti, 2022.
Available in English, Polish & French on Amazon.

The Little Botswana Boy, Feathered Friends, 2022.
Available in English on Amazon.

Follow The Little Botswana Boy on Instagram :
@thelittlebotswanaboy

Legal deposit : September 2024.
D/2024/Magdalena Collet, editor.

Made in the USA
Monee, IL
17 December 2024

74338987R00029